Schaum

(Early Elementary)

Masters of Technic

Primer Level

Technic etudes with emphasis on melody

Compiled, edited and arranged by Jeff Schaum and Wesley Schaum

FOREWORD

Numerous concert pianists and teachers were famous for their insights and development of successful piano technic, particularly during the 1800's. This series of books gives students an exposure to the rich variety of this technic heritage along with the benefits.

Primer Level contains 39 short exercises by 12 different master technic composers. Emphasis is placed on the ***melodic aspect of technic*** for greater student appeal. The exercises are purposely condensed, modified or transposed to achieve equal hand development.

Hand positions are purposely varied to avoid rigid five-finger position habits. Accidentals and different key signatures give students experience in various hand positions with black keys. Circles are placed around important finger numbers to show different hand positions.

The exercises are arranged in order of increasing difficulty. While becoming more challenging, the exercises complement the progress in a method book at the same level.

See the Composer Sources and Index on page 24

PRACTICE SUGGESTIONS

To derive the most benefit, attention should be given to how the exercises are practiced. ***Careful listening*** is necessary in order to hear a good balance between the accompaniment and the melody. The accompaniment should not be too loud. It is also important to listen for ***steady and accurate rhythm***, and to make sure each finger plays equally loud, especially the 4th and 5th fingers.

Each exercise should be practiced four or five times daily, starting at a slow tempo and gradually increasing the speed as proficiency improves. Several previously learned exercises should be reviewed each week as part of regular practice.

Schaum Publications, Inc. • 10235 N. Port Washington Rd. • Mequon, WI 53092
www.schaumpiano.net

© Copyright 2004 by Schaum Publications, Inc., Mequon, Wisconsin
International Copyright Secured • All Rights Reserved • Printed in U.S.A.
ISBN-13: 978-1-62906-084-2

Warning: The reproduction of any part of this publication without prior written consent of Schaum Publications, Inc. is prohibited by U.S. Copyright Law and subject to penalty. This prohibition includes all forms of printed media (including any method of photocopy), all forms of electronic media (including computer images), all forms of film media (including filmstrips, transparencies, slides and movies), all forms of sound recordings (including cassette tapes and compact disks), and all forms of video media (including video tapes and DVD).

Cramer • 3-finger study

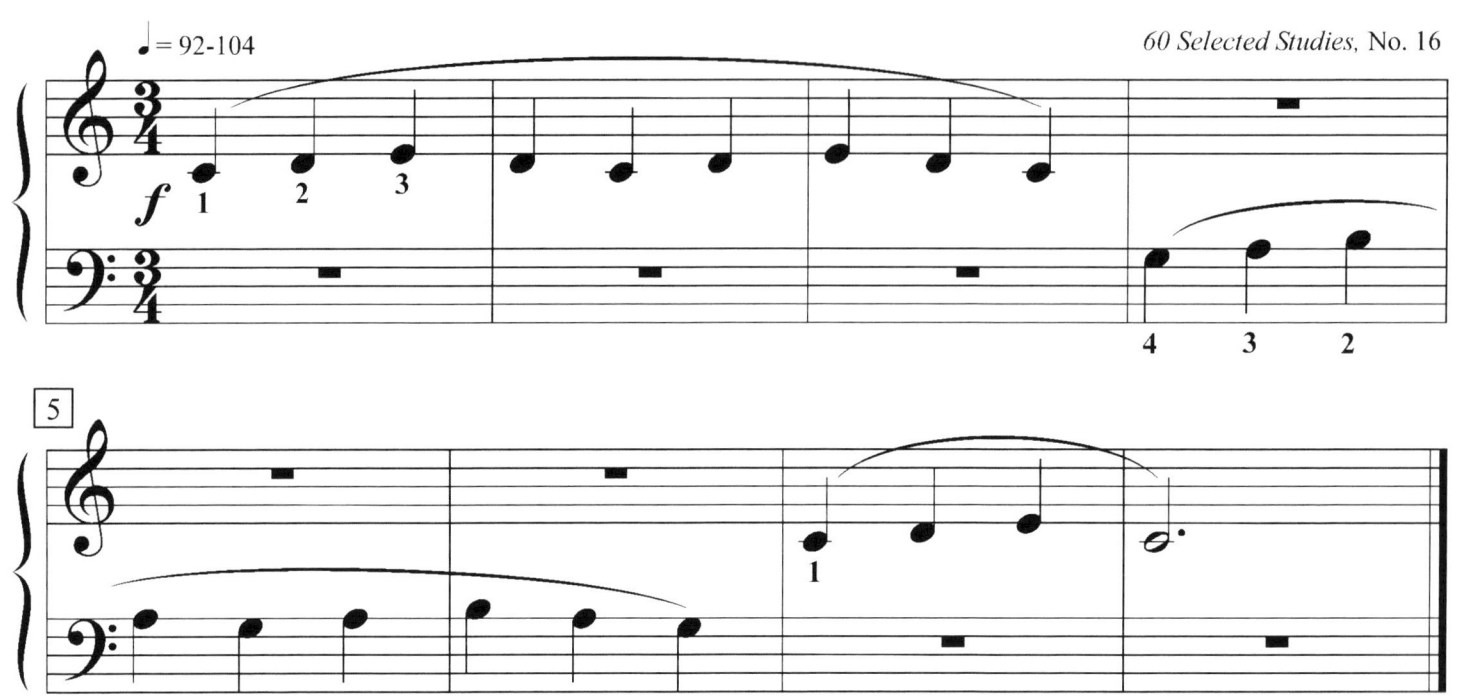

Wolff • Imitations for 3-fingers

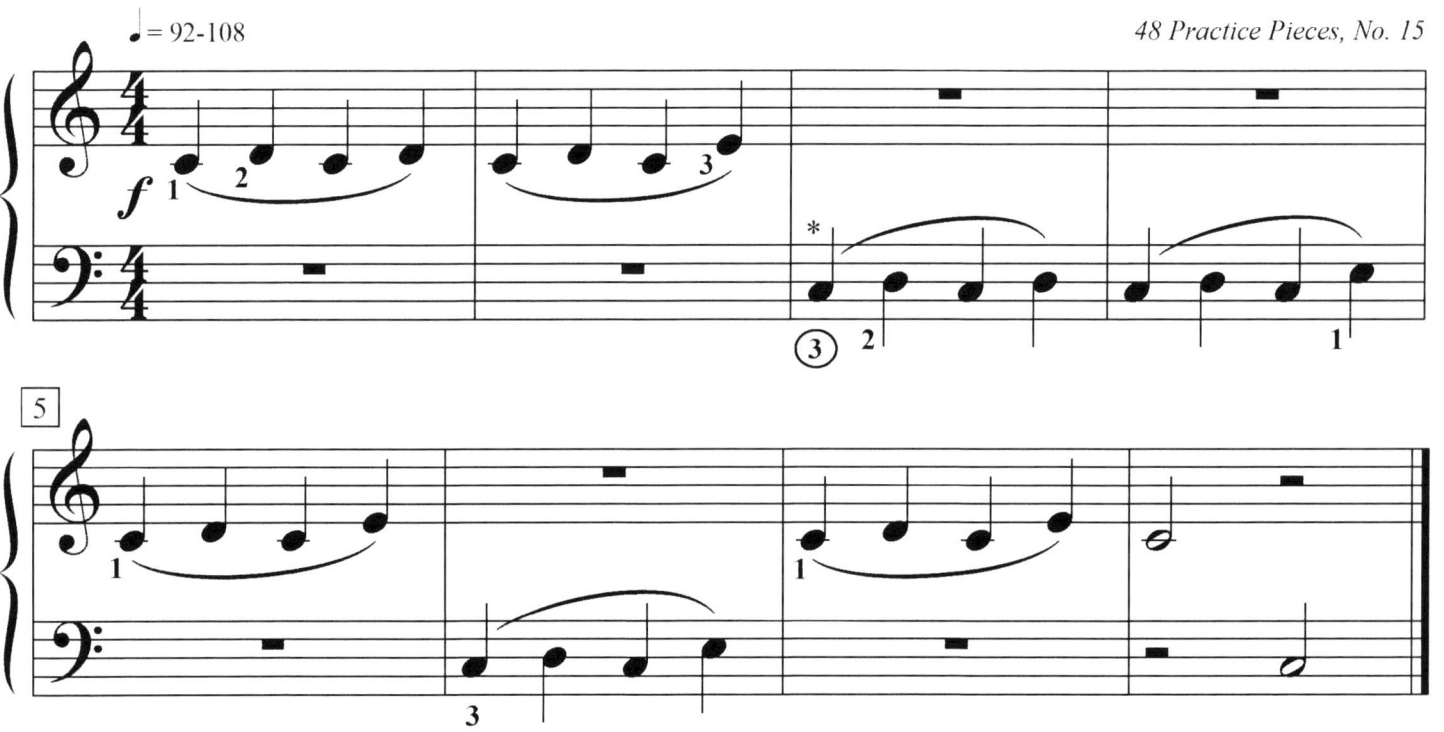

* This note is bass C, one octave below middle C.
A circle around a finger number shows a different hand position.

Krause • *5-finger study*

Krause • *4-finger exercise*

* Treble C (one octave above Middle-C).
The circle around the finger number shows a different hand position.

Burgmüller • D minor study

Op. 100, No. 20

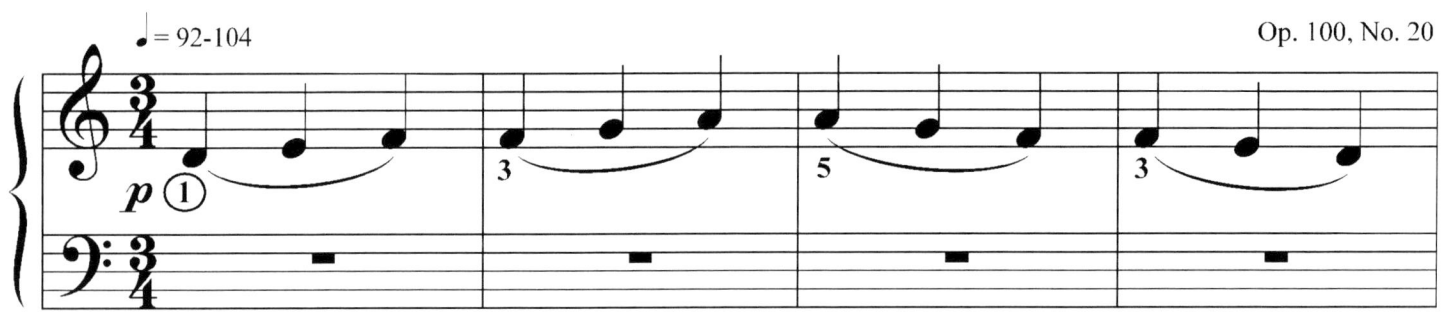
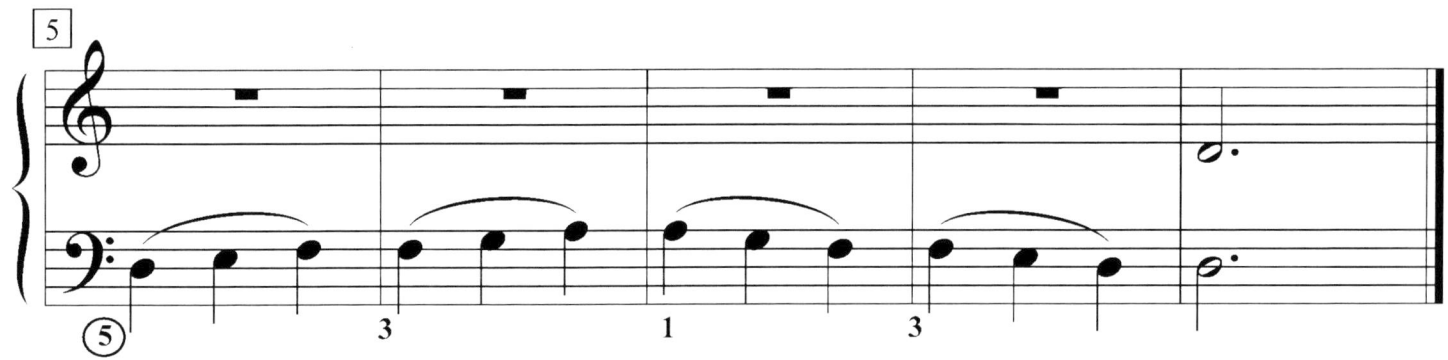

Cramer • Alternating hand patterns

60 Selected Studies, No. 1

Beringer • *C major 5-finger etude*

Daily Technical Studies, No. 75B

Beringer • *4-note groups*

Daily Technical Studies, No. 67B

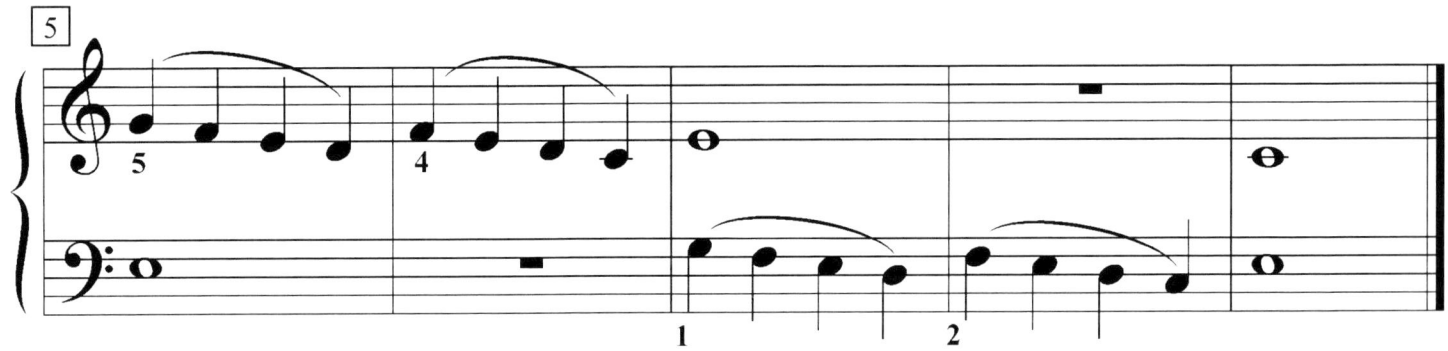

Wolff • *4-finger patterns*

48 Practice Pieces, No. 20

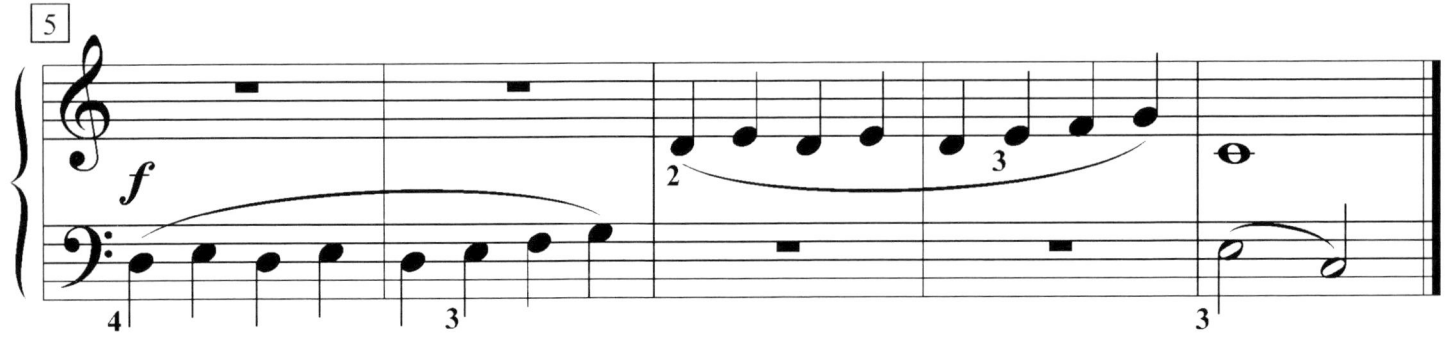

Beringer • Repeated note patterns

Daily Technical Studies, No. 61B

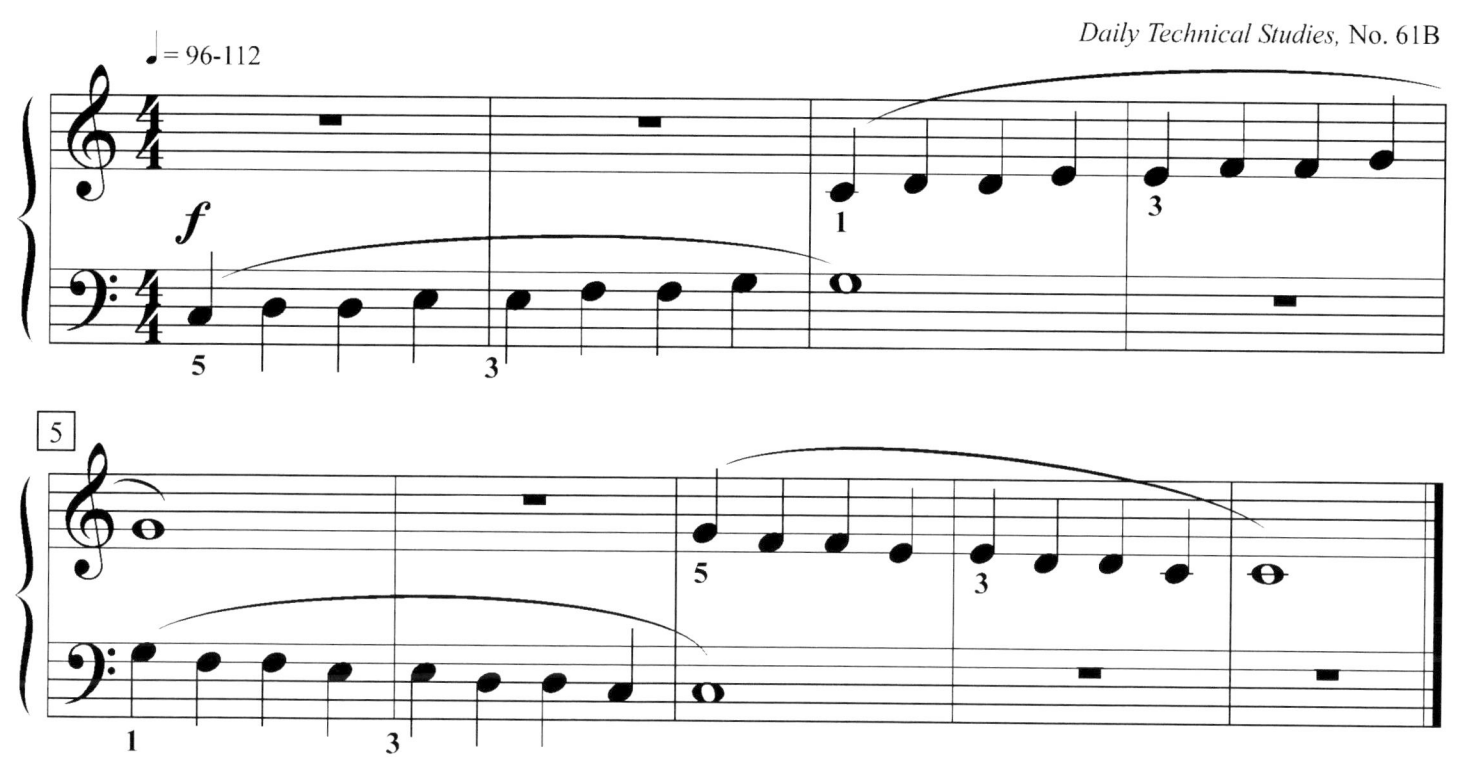

Loeschhorn • F major study

Op.169, No. 3

Cramer • F major etude

60 Selected Studies, No. 9

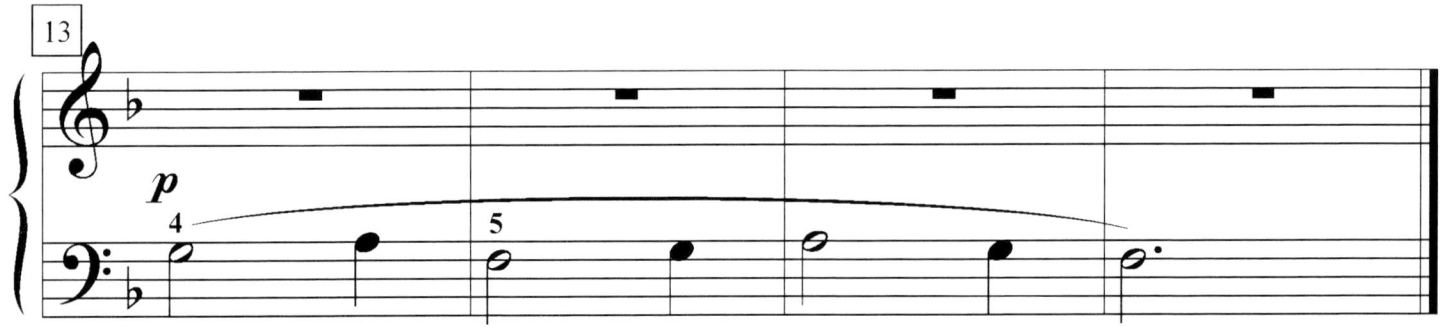

Czerny • *3-finger patterns with F-sharp*

Krause • *3-note groups with F-sharp*

Beringer • *Major and minor 5-finger etude*

Daily Technical Studies, No. 4A

Hanon • Upward pattern

Hanon • Downward pattern

Czerny • F major etude

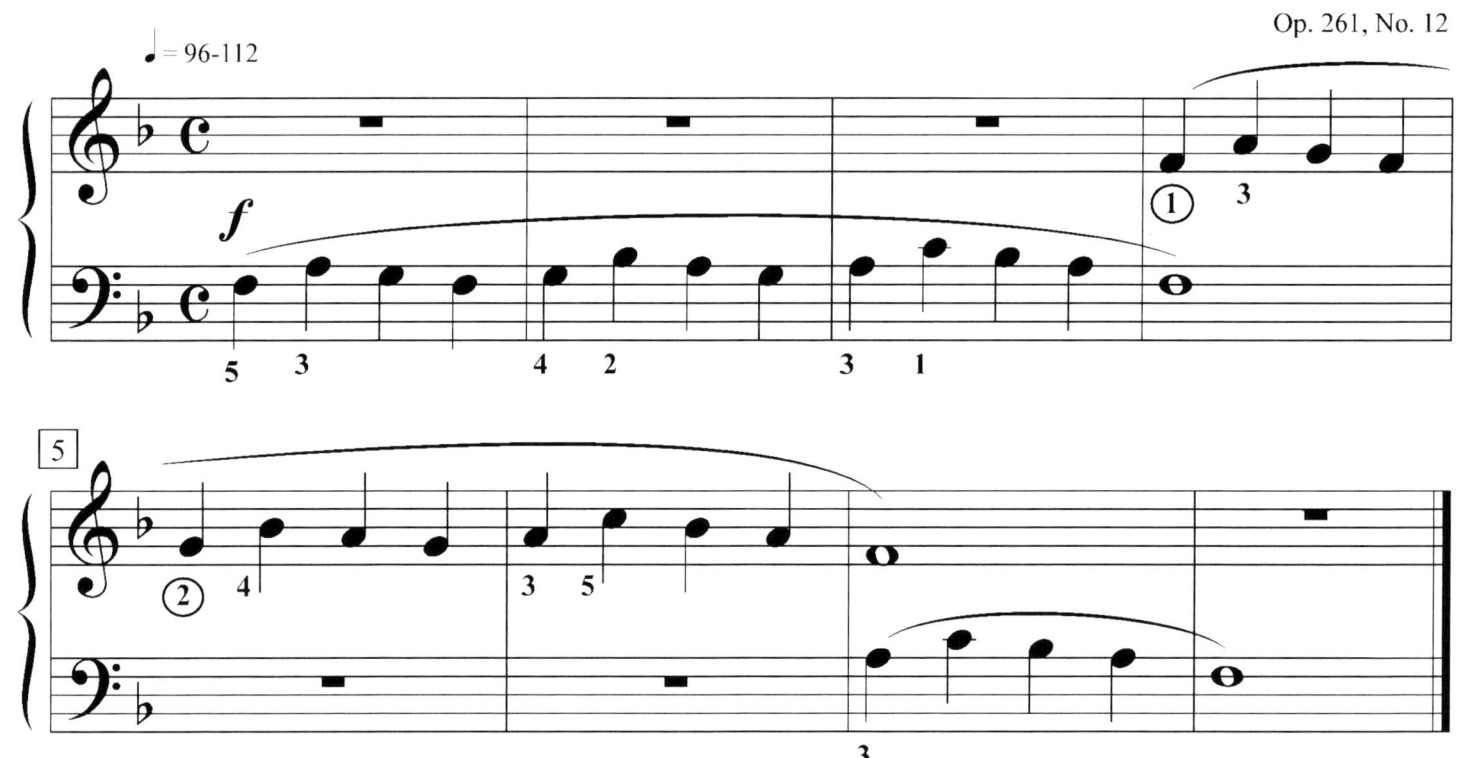

Krause • F major 5-finger etude

Concone · G major scale configuration

Op. 37, No. 11

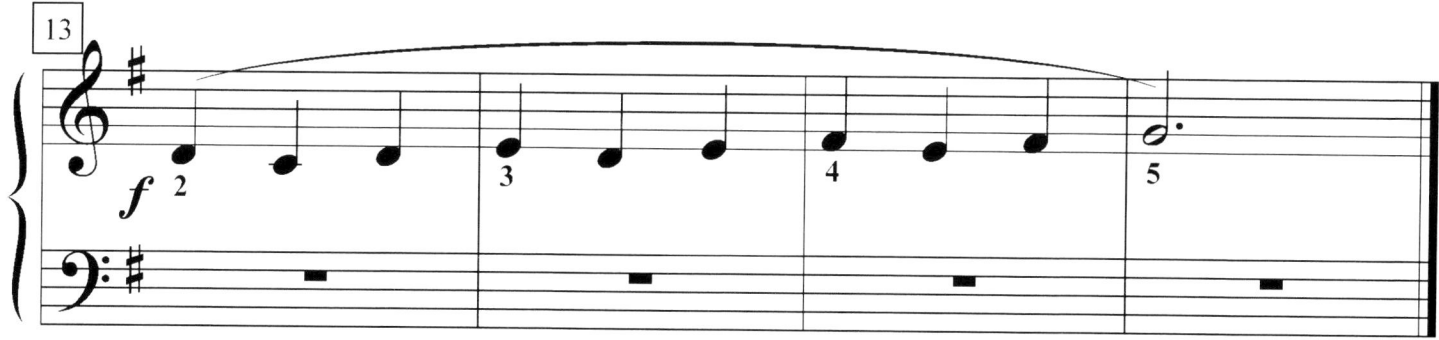

Loeschhorn • G major 5-finger patterns

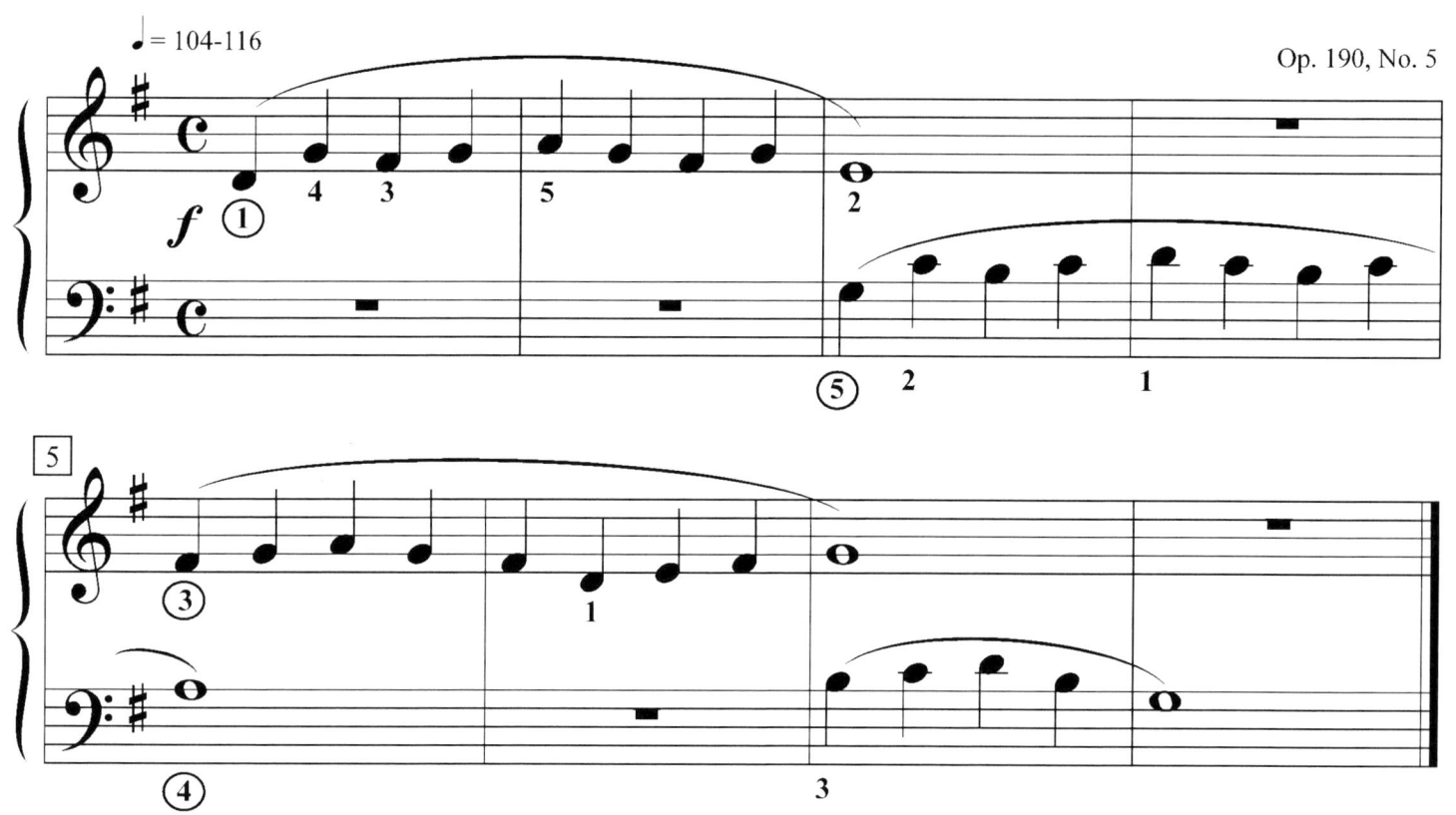

Beringer • E minor exercise

Czerny • *5-finger patterns*

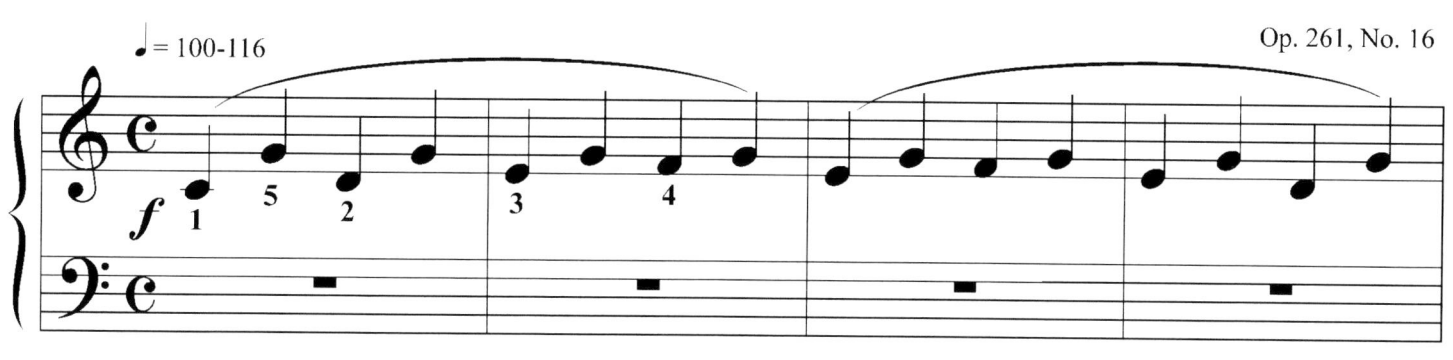
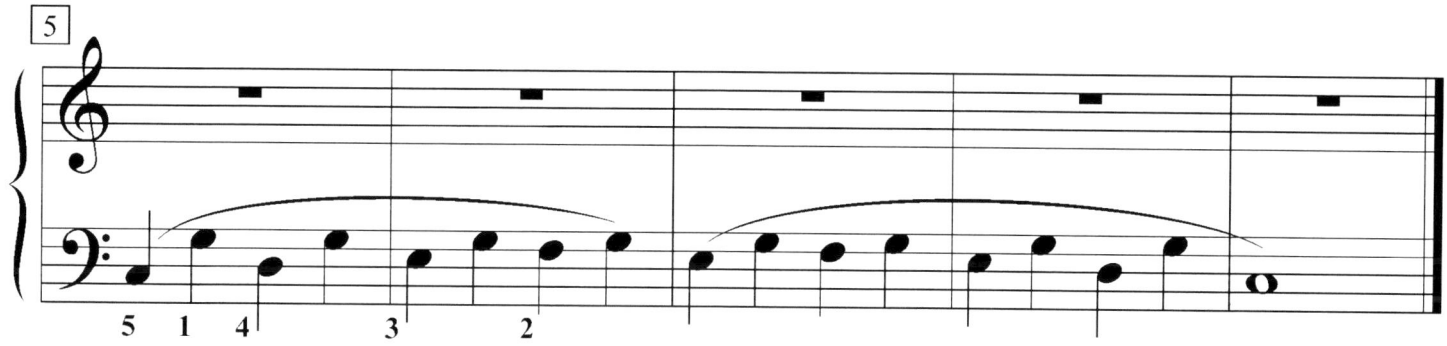

Krause • *Mixed interval study*

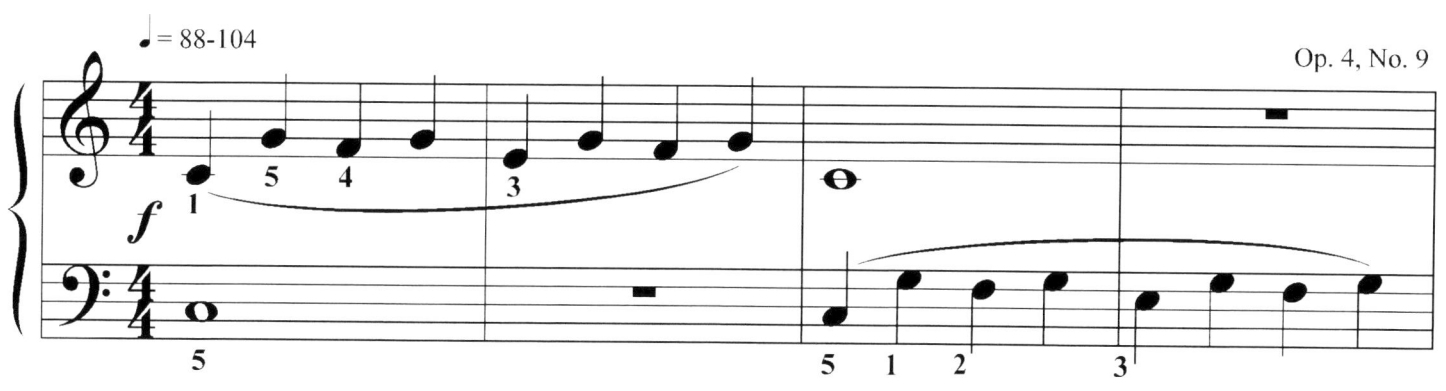
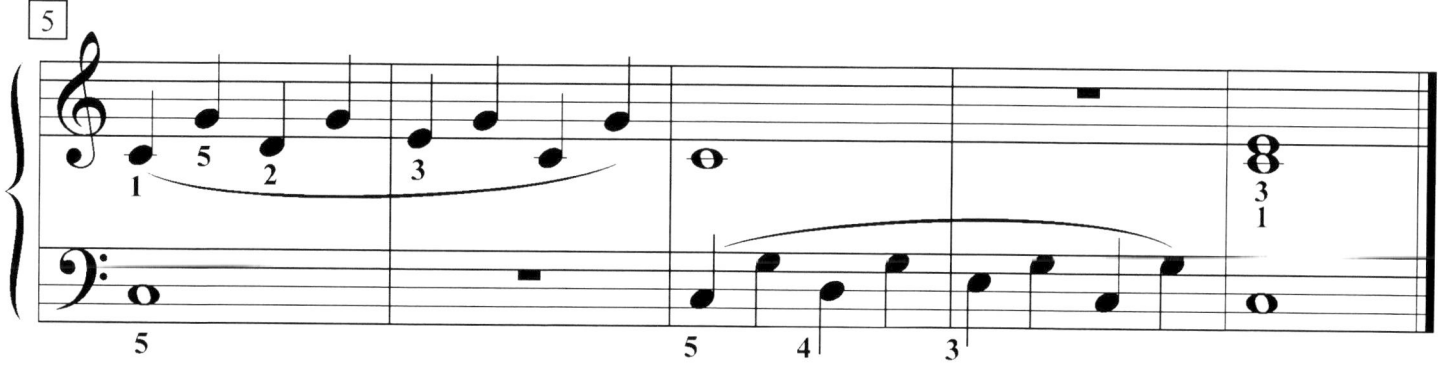

Loeschhorn • G major melody

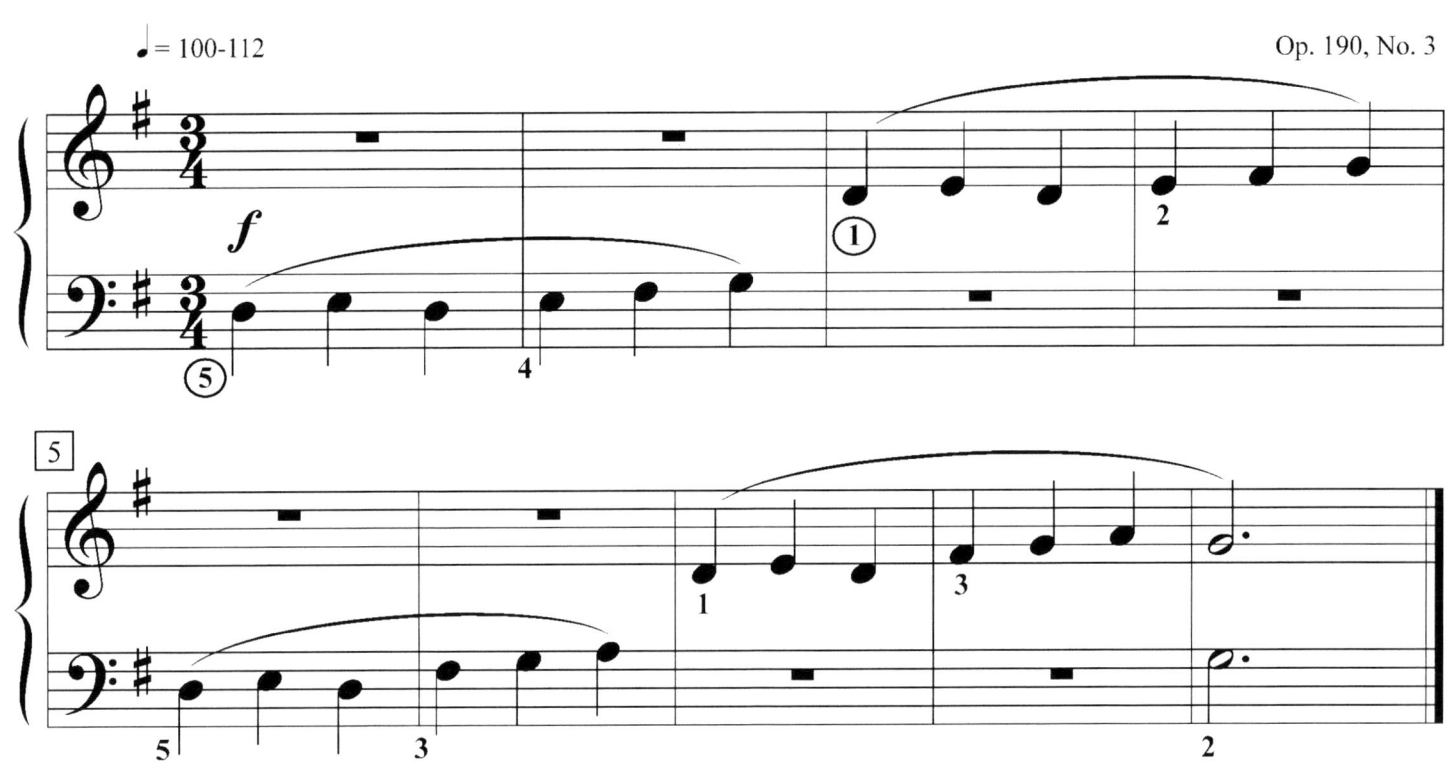

Wolff • F major 4-finger study

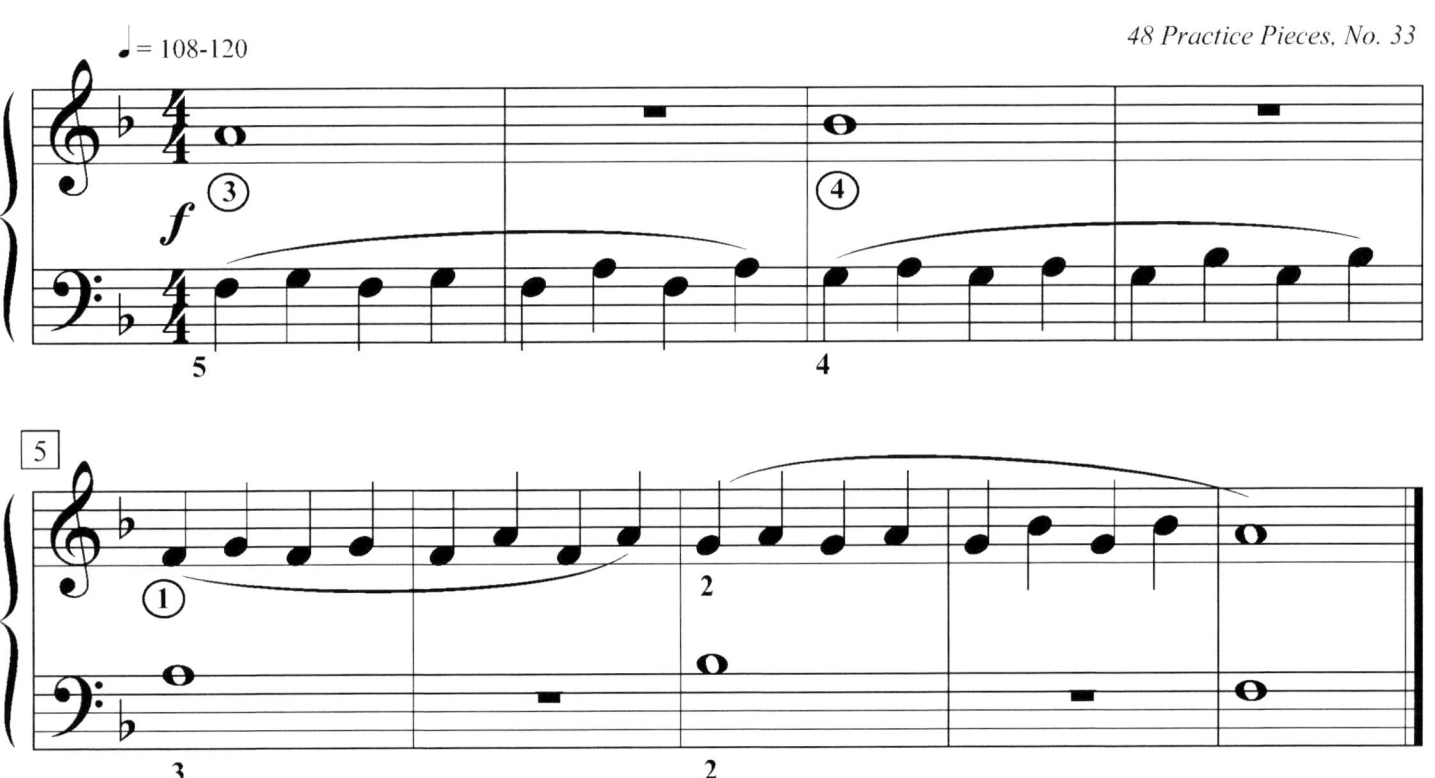

Krause • *Patterns in F major*

Op. 4, No. 2

Cramer • Imitation study

60 Selected Studies, No. 1

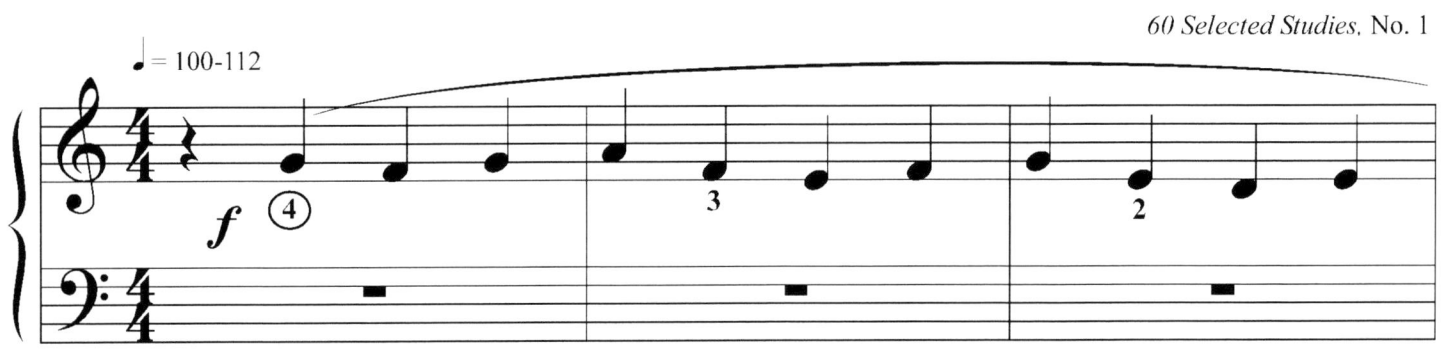

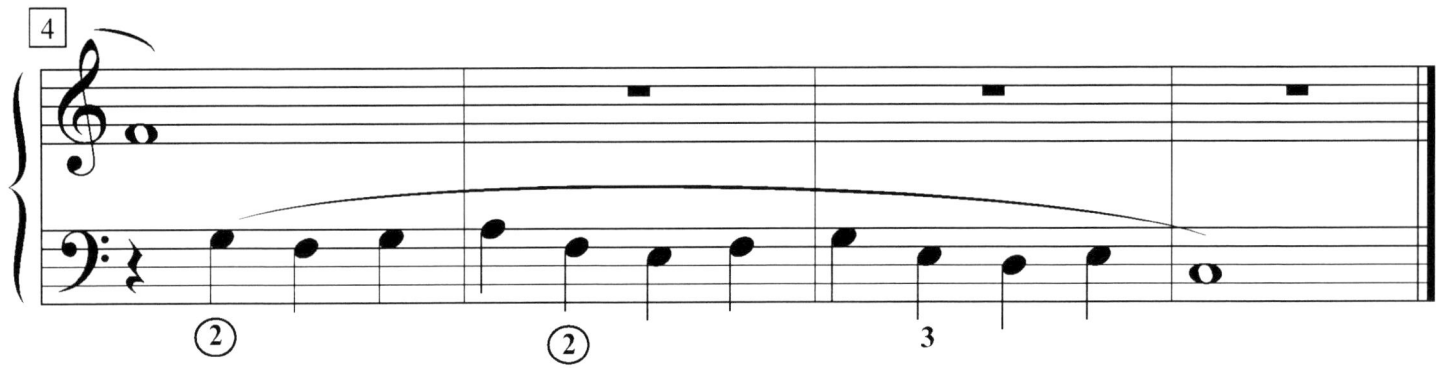

Cramer • G major pattern

60 Selected Studies, No. 22

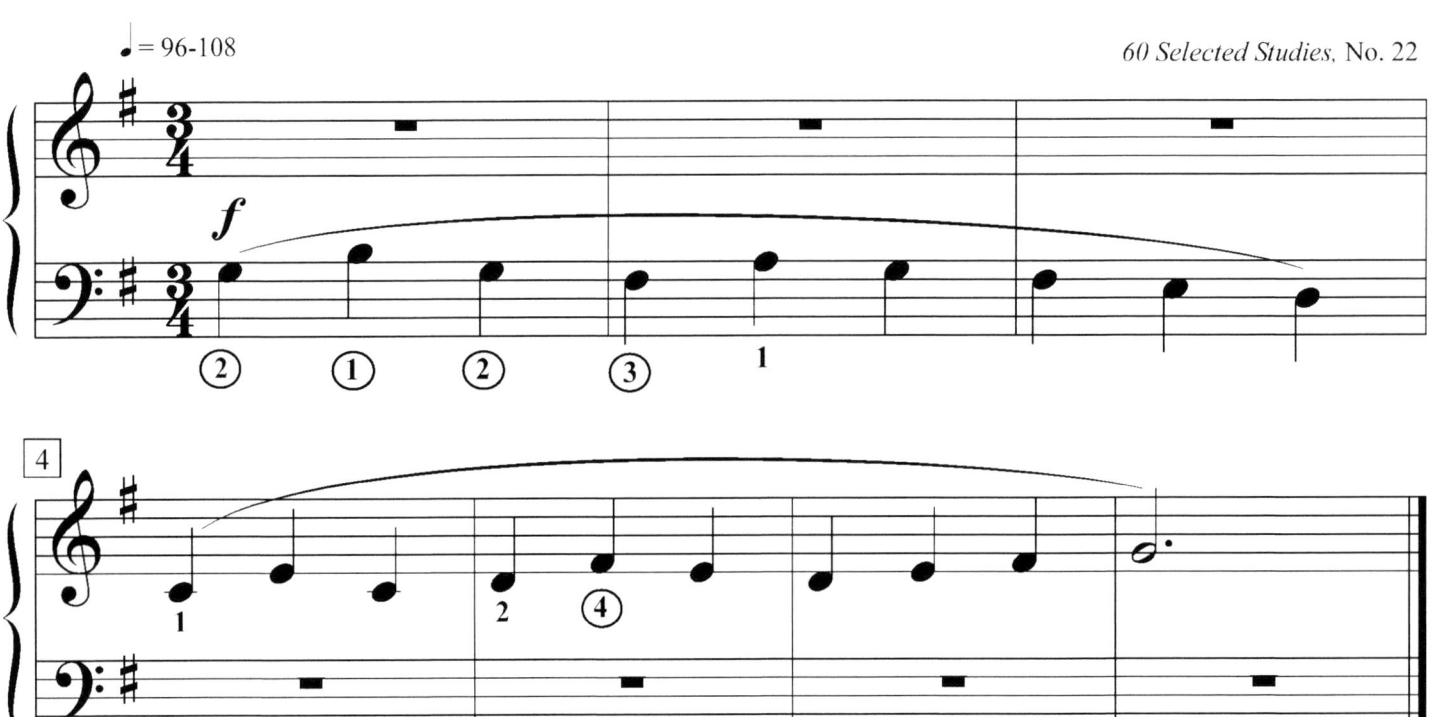

Biehl • *Exercise without using thumb*

♩ = 88-104

Op. 139, No. 11

Loeschhorn • *Minor key study with staccato*

♩ = 100-112

Op. 190, No. 2

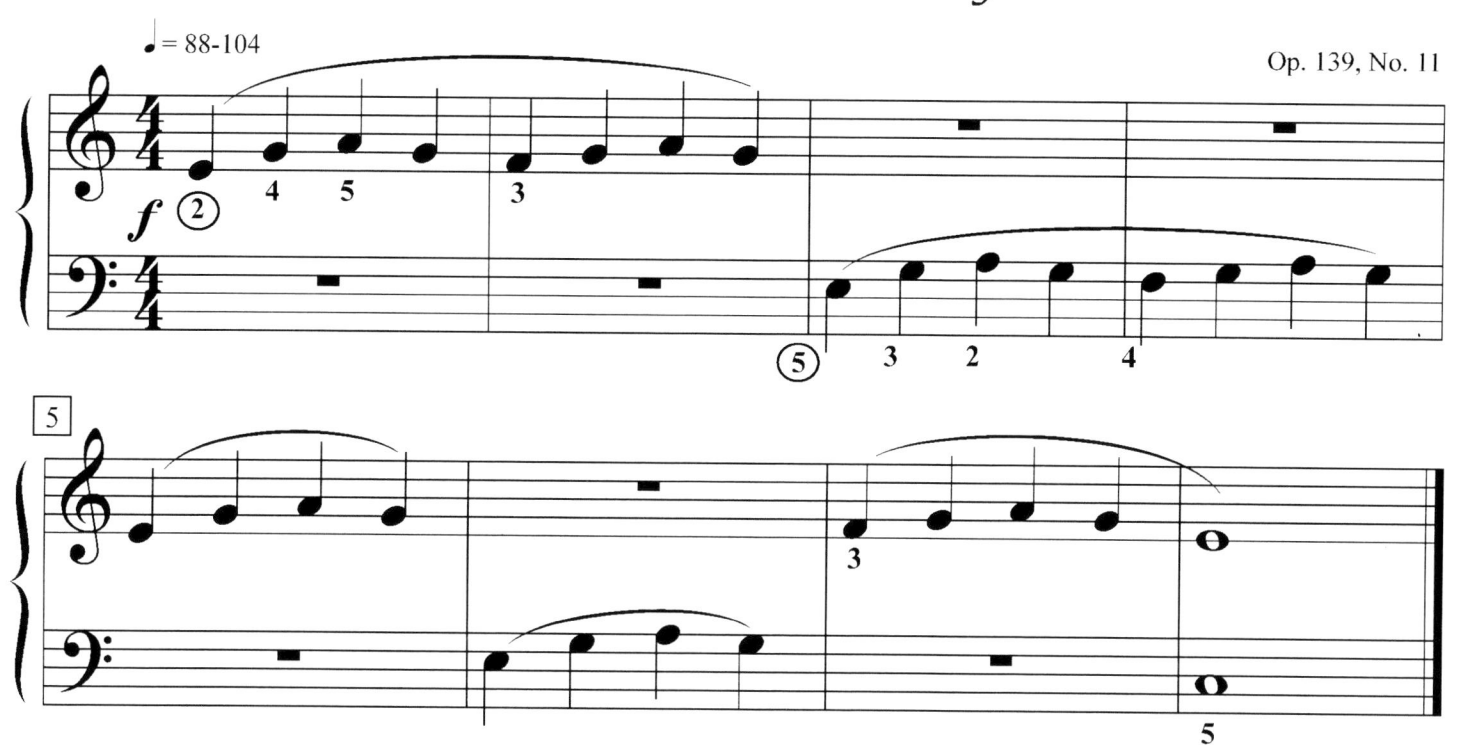

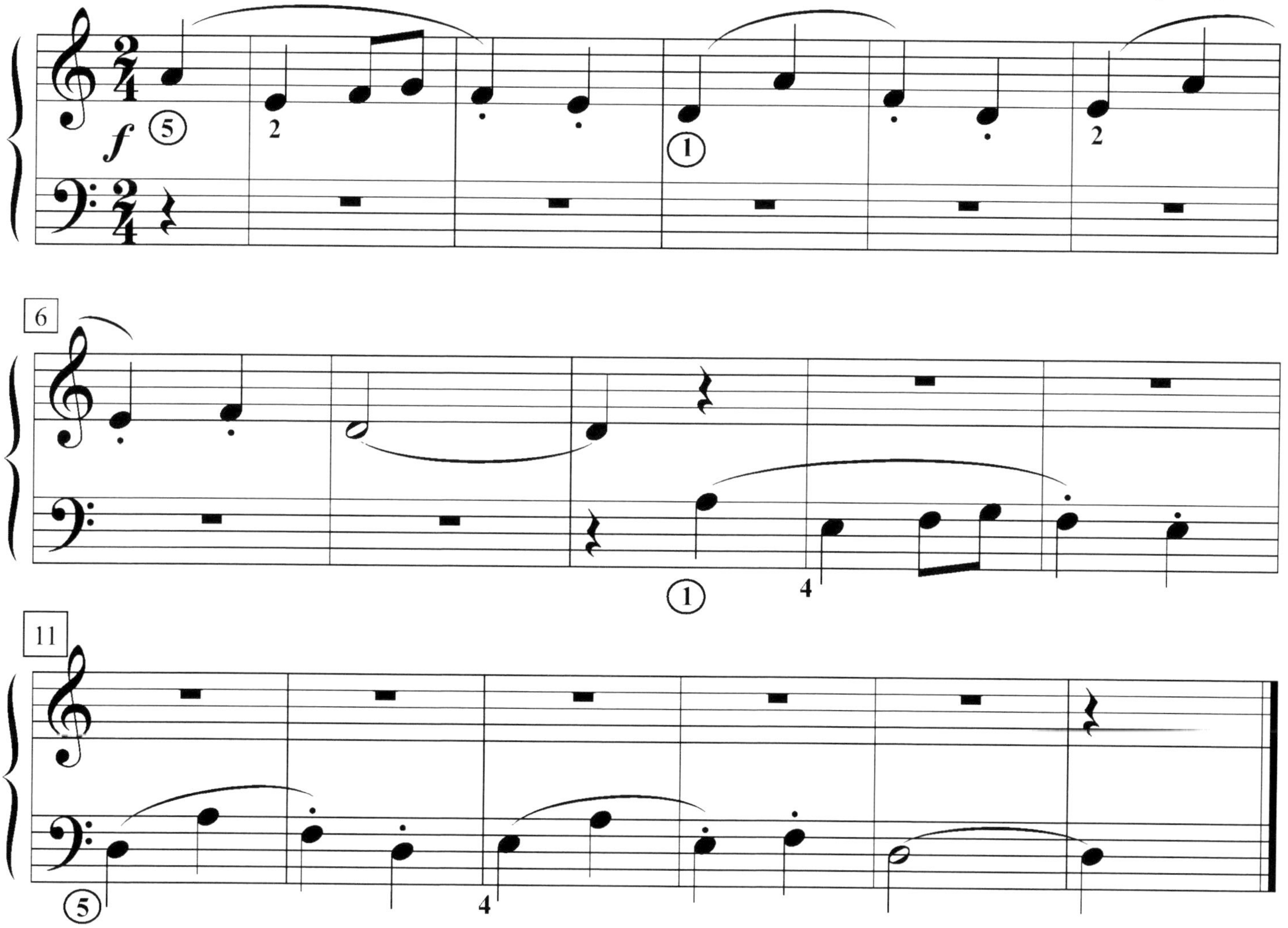

Czerny • *Hand compression with staccato*

♩ = 80-96

Op. 261, No. 17

Biehl • *Hand extension*

♩ = 100-116

Op. 139, No. 6

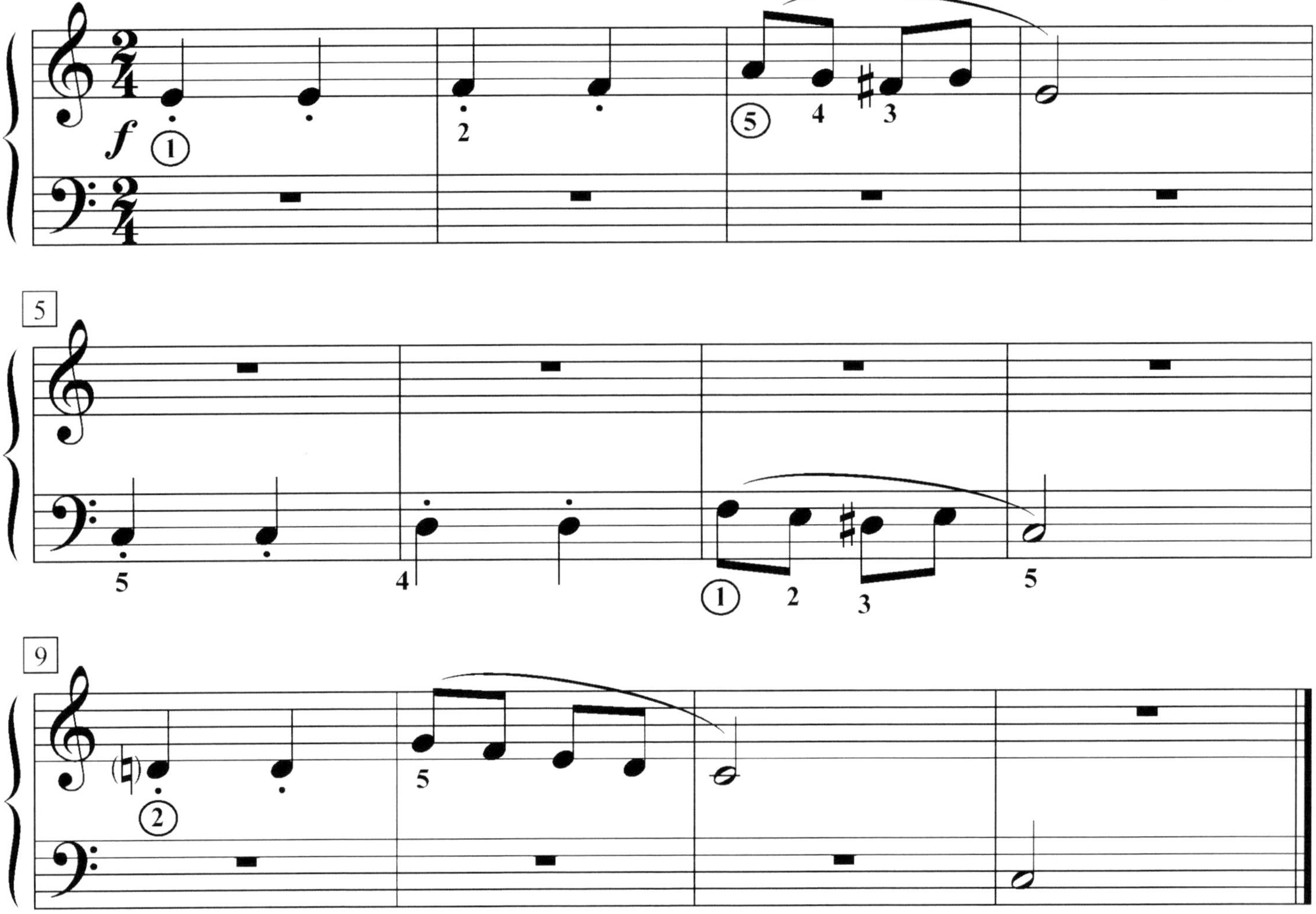

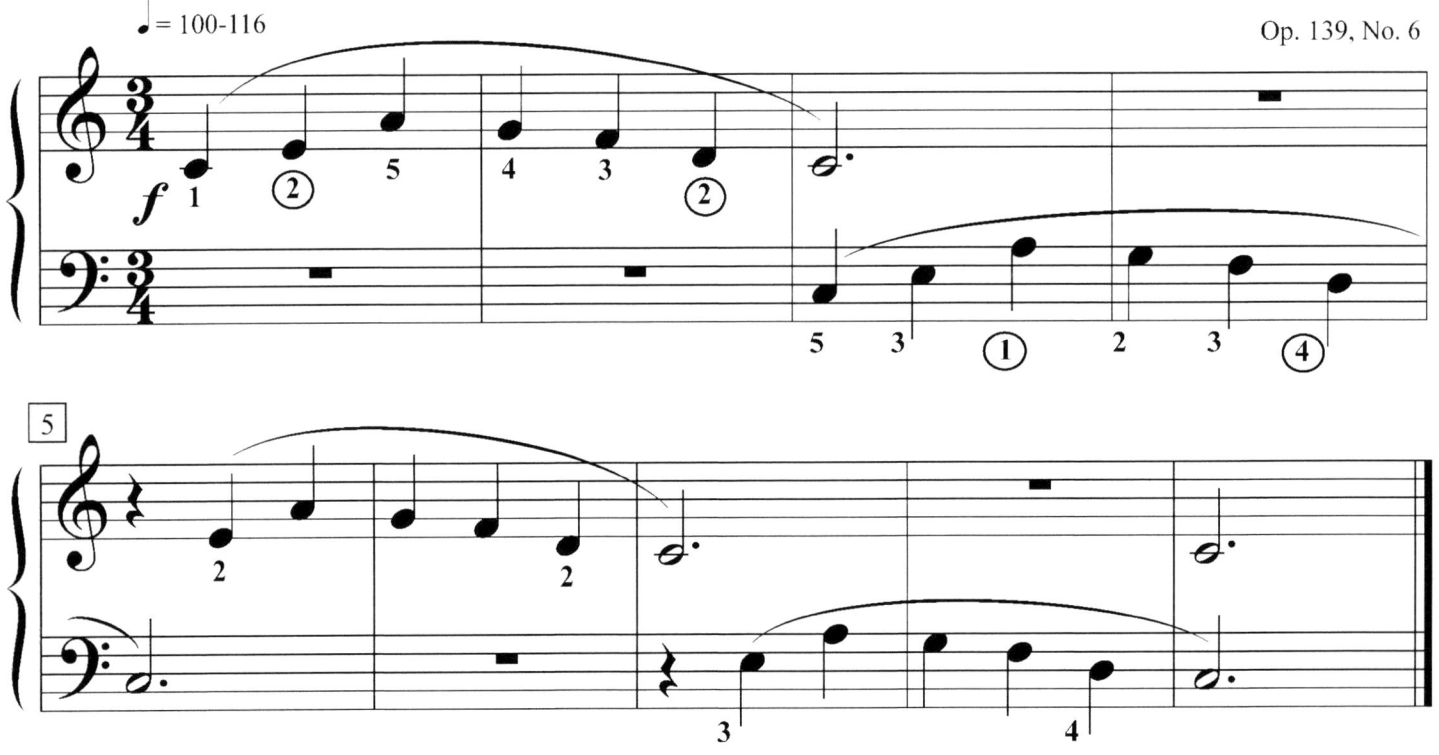

Brauer • *Hand extension*

♩ = 100-112

Op. 15, No. 10

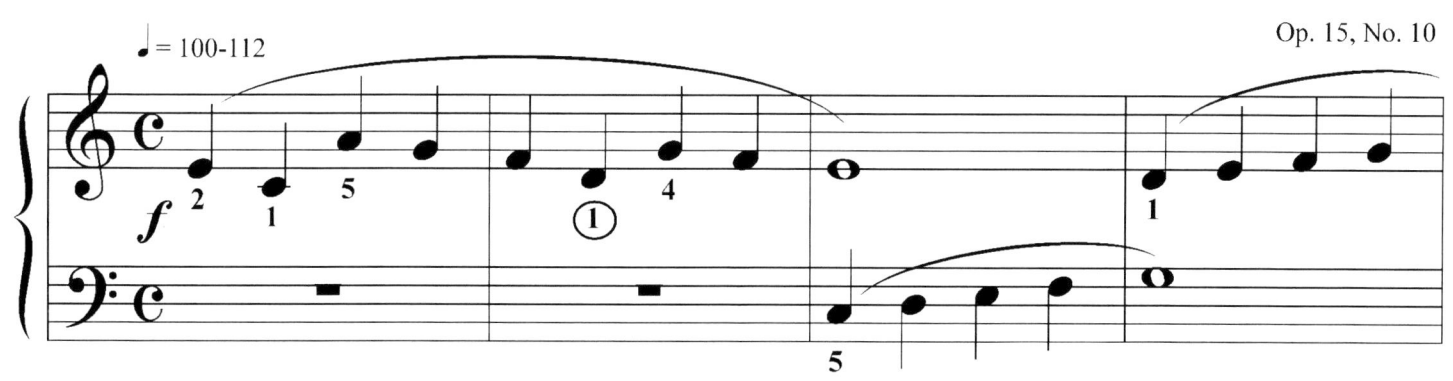

Streabbog • *D major hand position with sharps*

♩ = 96-108

Op. 262, No. 2

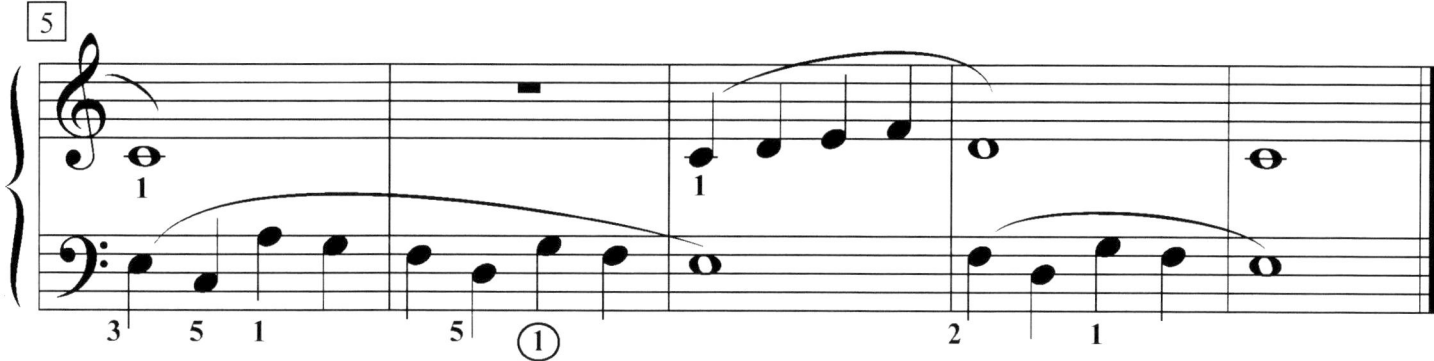

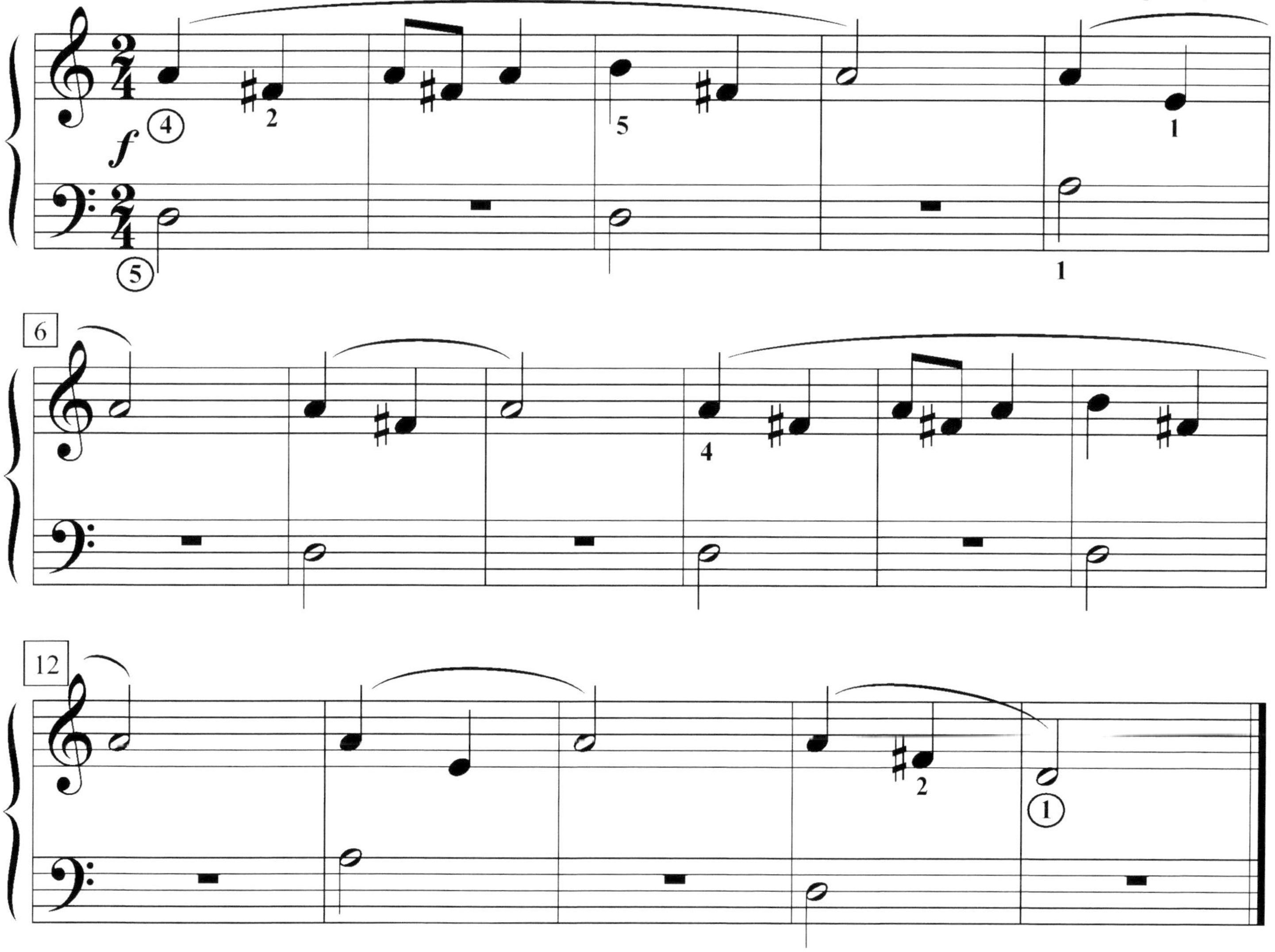

Concone • Short chromatic study

Op. 37, No. 1

Czerny • 2/4 patterns with 8th notes

Op. 261, No. 13

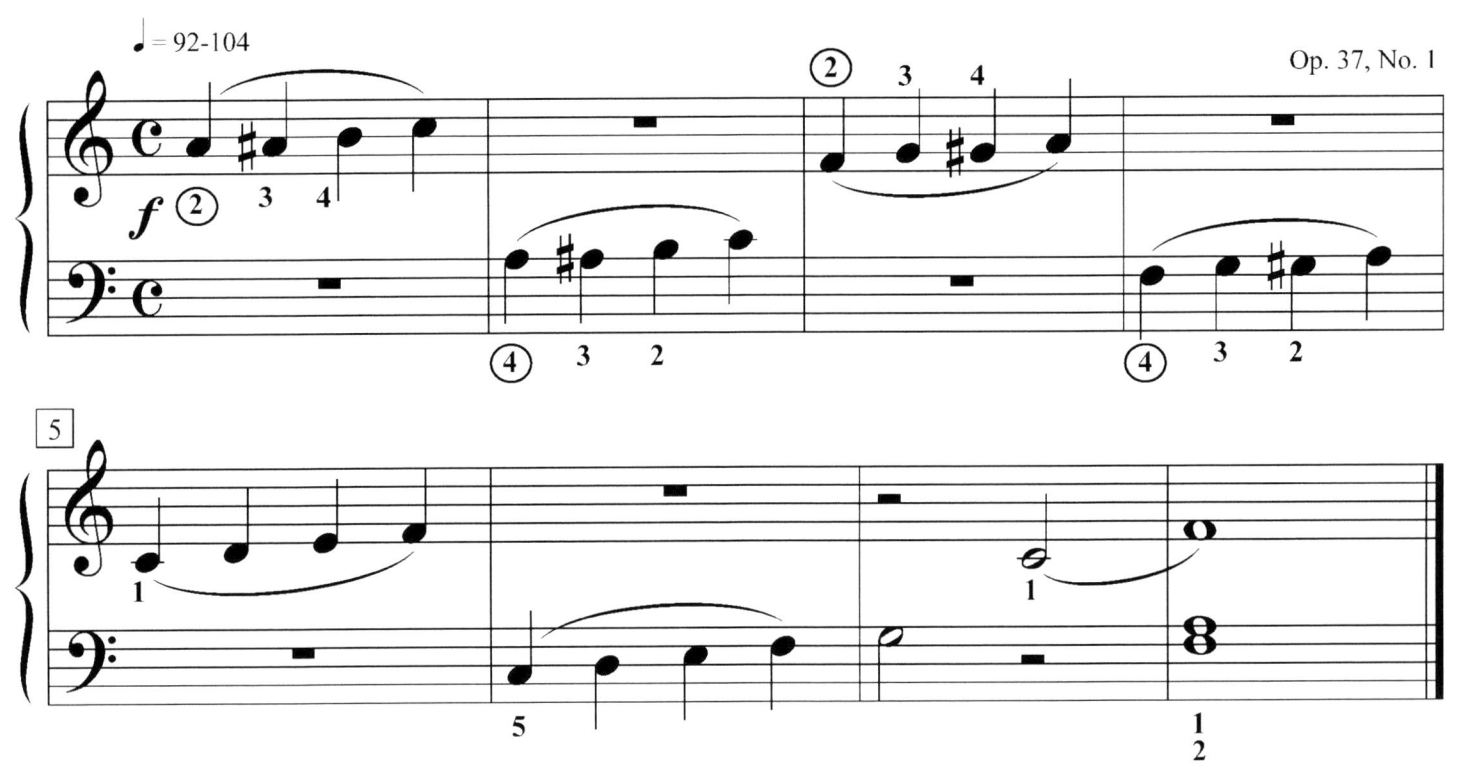

Wolff • 4-finger study in 2/4 time

♩ = 54-63

48 Practice Pieces, No. 33

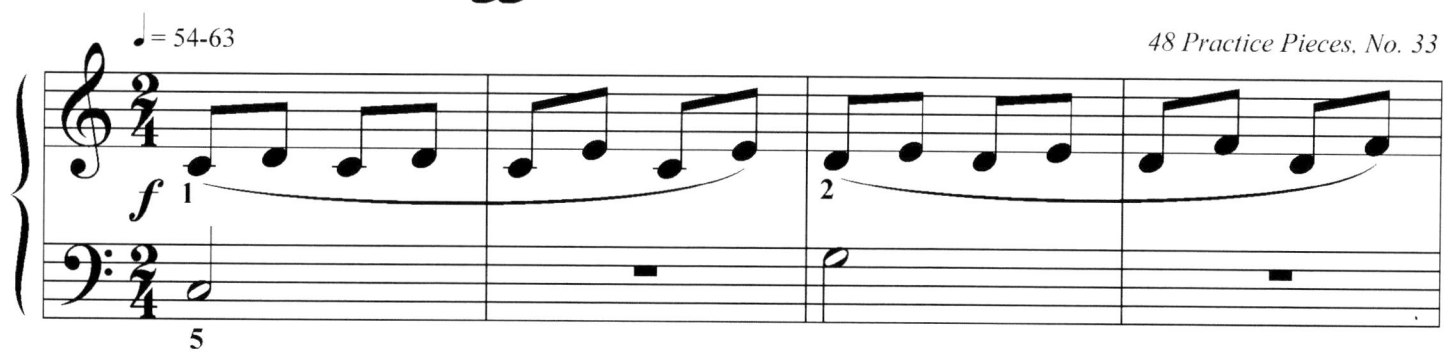

Burgmüller • Broken chords in extended hand position

♩ = 96-112

Op. 100, No. 21

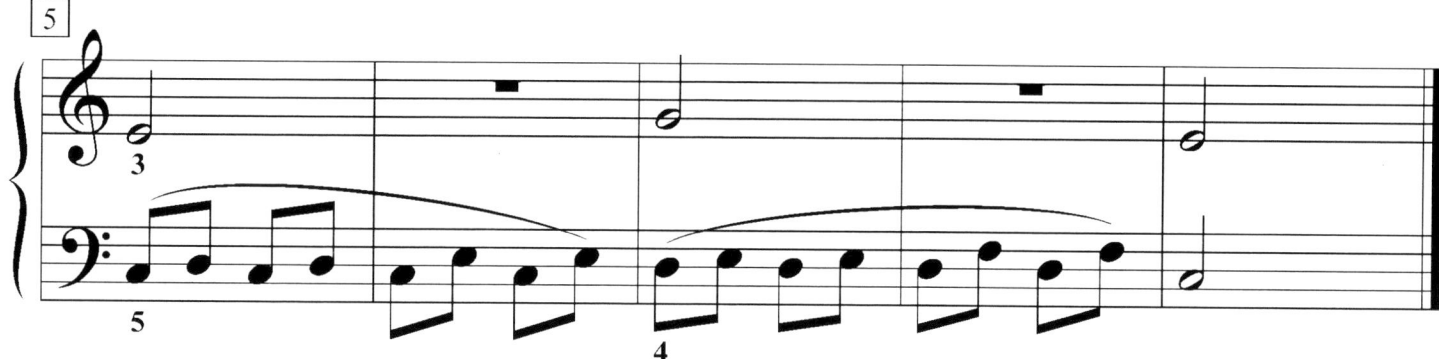

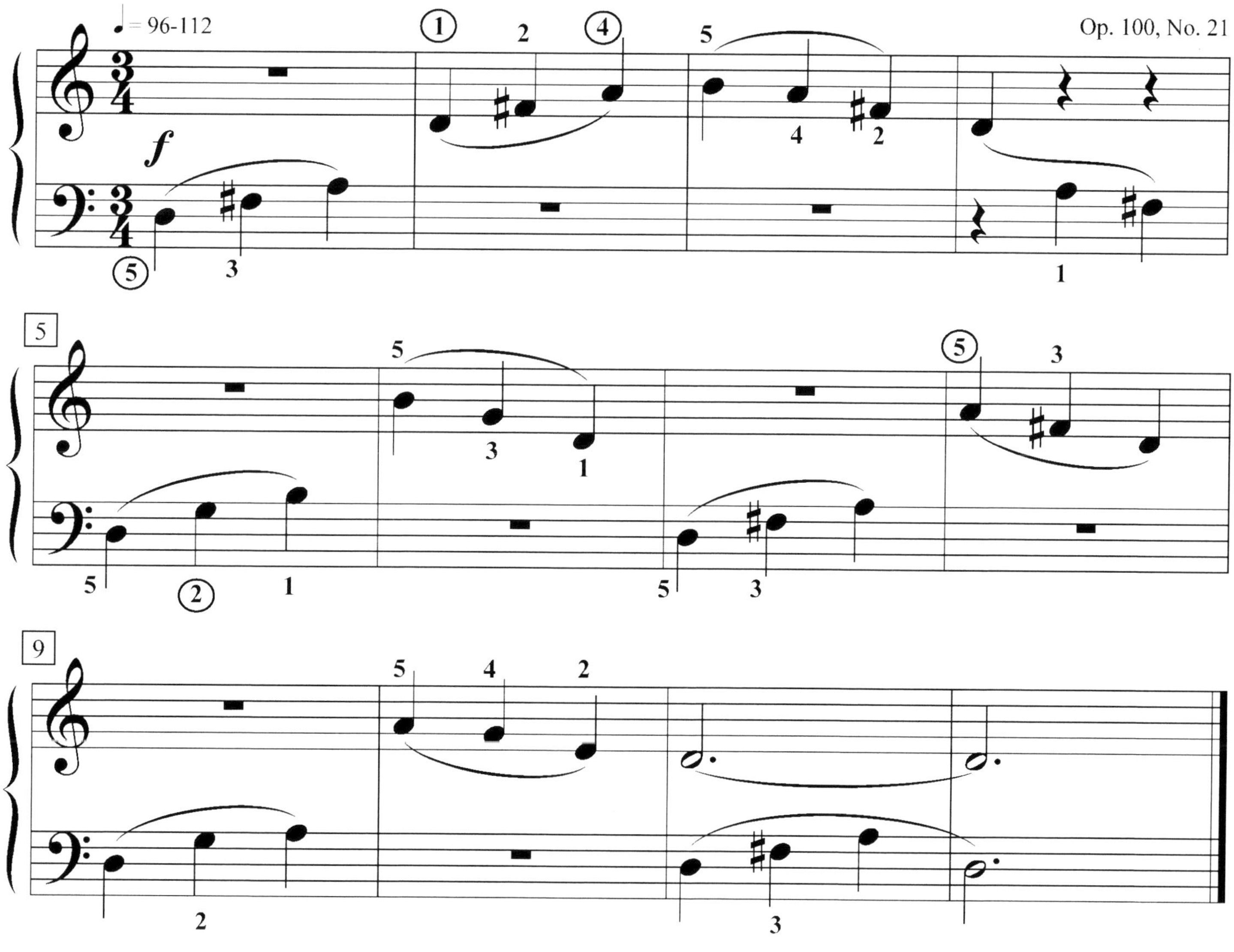

Composer Sources and Index

Beringer, Oscar (1844-1922) Germany
    pg. 5, 6, 7, 10, 14 .... *Daily Technical Studies*, No. 4A, 61B, 66B, 67B, 75B

Biehl, Albert (1835-1899) Germany
    pg. 19, 20 .... Op. 139, No. 6, 11

Brauer, Friedrich (1806-1898) Germany
    pg. 21 .... Op. 15, No. 10

Burgmüller, Johann Friedrich (1806-1874) Germany
    pg. 4, 23 .... Op. 100, No. 20, 21

Concone, Giuseppe (1801-1861) Italy
    pg. 13, 22 .... Op. 137 No. 1, 11

Cramer, Johann Baptist (1771-1858) Germany
    pg. 2, 4, 8, 18 .... *60 Selected Studies*, No. 1, 9, 16, 22

Czerny, Carl (1791-1857) Austria
    pg. 9, 12, 15, 20, 22 .... Op. 261, No. 8, 12, 13, 16, 17

Hanon, Charles Louis (1819-1900) France
    pg. 11 .... *Virtuoso Pianist*, No. 21

Krause, Anton (1834-1907) Germany
    pg. 9, 12, 15, 17 .... Op. 4, No. 2, 9, 15, 18
    pg. 3 .... Op. 25, No. 5, 21

Loeschhorn, Carl Albert (1819-1905) Germany
    pg. 7 .... Op. 169, No. 3
    pg. 14, 16, 19 .... Op. 190, No. 2, 3, 5

Streabbog, Louis (pseudonym of Gobbaerts) (1835-1886) Belgium
    pg. 21 .... Op. 262, No. 2

Wolff, Bernhard (1835-1906) Germany
    pg. 2, 6, 16, 23 .... *48 Practice Pieces* ("Little Pischna"), No. 15, 20, 33